Stripes & Plaids

Table of Contents

Using Stripes & Plaids 2

Willy-Nilly 7

Plaid Maze 10

Patriotic Bouquets 15

Riding Around...................19

Strips & Squares 24

Cardinals Rule 28

Flower Paths 33

Nosegay Stars....................38

Starring Stripes.................45

Framed in Plaid Flowers 49

Firecracker Basket 55

Preparing Bias Strips 60

Matching Stripes at Mitered Corners 62

Meet the Designers

Sue Harvey

Sue Harvey and Sandra L. Hatch have been working together in the quilting world for many years. Sandra has been editing quilting magazines for more than 20 years. Sue has been working with her as the senior editor for *Quilter's World* since 2003. Before that time, they worked together on other quilting publications, including several previous books for House of White Birches.

Sandra comes from a sewing background with lots of experience and years of garment making. She has also been a public-school sewing teacher. On the other hand, Sue has come to quiltmaking without sewing experience and the rules that go with it. She likes to say that she "doesn't know how to sew, only quilt." Their "right-way/wrong-way" styles have contributed to many lively designing sessions.

Because of their differing backgrounds, they have found that their book collaborations result in a wide variety of projects. In this book their goal is to give quilters the freedom to use plaids and stripes in quilts without letting the fabrics create cutting and stitching problems. They also hope to encourage more traditional quiltmakers to forget the sewing rules for using these wonderful fabrics and, instead, use stripes and plaids with abandon to add zip to their quilts.

Sandra L. Hatch

Using Stripes & Plaids

Break the rules of matching to make exciting quilts full of action.

If you came to quilting from a sewing background, you have learned that plaids or stripes were hard to use. When purchasing these fabrics for clothing, more fabric is always required for matching lines at seams. The cutting process is more tedious because every piece must be matched to its adjoining piece during the pattern layout process. For some people, this is too scary, and so many seamstresses avoid using plaids and stripes in garments.

If you came to quilting with no sewing background, you never learned any of these rules, so you can make your own. What we have learned is that there is not really a right or wrong way to work with plaids and stripes—they can be used like any other fabric. There should be no rules except your own. Of course, the result should be a project that is pleasing to the eye with your best workmanship.

Woven Versus Printed Stripes & Plaids

Lengthwise and crosswise grain lines are easy to identify using any thread in a woven plaid or stripe fabric. Theoretically, this should make cutting individual pieces in the direction of the stripe or along a specific line in the plaid very easy. The size of the lines and the distance between them determines how easy this can be.

Trying to cut or stitch on a tiny line proves nearly impossible, and quite tedious, even with woven plaids and stripes.

It is more desirable to try to cut the fabric so that the stitching line falls between the lines rather than right on the edge of a line, especially on a striped fabric where the lines run only one way.

If you are really aiming for exact-line stitching throughout, mistakes will really stand out.

Printed plaids and stripes are printed onto previously woven fabric. The obvious line of the

Cut with the print

Cut with the grain

HOUSE OF WHITE BIRCHES, BERNE, INDIANA 46711 WWW.WHITEBIRCHES.COM

print is often not the true grain line. This creates the need to make a choice—do you go with the true grain line and use pieces in which the print line doesn't align with the edge of the piece, or do you go with the print so it aligns with the edges and handle potential off-grain or bias edges with care? This decision may make a big difference in the look of your quilt.

Creating a Style of Quilt

The style of quilt that you choose to make should also be considered when deciding how to cut and use plaids and stripes. Matching grain lines creates a more rigid-looking quilt—one with very little movement. The fabric lines stop or align neatly at the edge of a piece or stop at a 45- or 90-degree angle and are then matched with

lines in the adjoining pieces. The eye does move along the lines, but always straight, never wavering from side to side. These quilts have a more formal or planned feel to them.

Matching grain lines also eliminates the ability to rotary-cut several layers at a time—each layer must be cut individually to ensure that the grain runs exactly with the edge of the quilt pieces. Quick quilts are out of the question.

Using pieces that are slightly off-grain gives a more casual, folk-art look to a quilt. Pieces that are very off-grain have a primitive look. These types of quilts are often seen

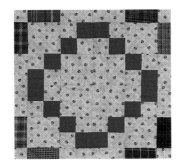

as appliqué quilts and pieced quilts made with homespun-style wovens. The pieces readily lend themselves to rotary-cutting through several layers at a time, making them much faster to construct.

Quilts made with off-grain stripe or plaid pieces benefit from the addition of fabrics that read as plain. These plain areas in an otherwise busy quilt slow the eye and regulate the movement from one place to another.

Solid, mottled and tonal fabrics are often used for this purpose. However, one-color or muted-color plaids or stripes can also give the effect of a solid fabric.

Using Stripes & Plaids in Borders

If using a plaid or stripe in the borders of a quilt, extra planning during the cutting process is extremely important. If you want a stripe or plaid to match at a mitered seam, the cutting direction is important.

Stripe borders may be cut either along the length or across the width as long as stripes are matched at the mitered corners.

It is important to select the same striped section and center it in each border strip to match at each corner.

For plaids, all the border strips must be cut along the length and stitched to the edges so that the same section of plaid matches at 45-degree angles at the corners.

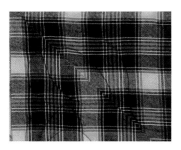

Plaids have a repeat of pattern—a square or rectangle in which the rows of color form one complete pattern. If folded in half lengthwise and then crosswise and the rows of colors and spaces match in both directions, the plaid is even. This makes matching easier. Uneven plaids will not match in both directions.

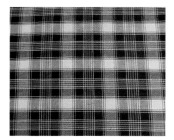 

Checks are even plaids. A true checked fabric is made of evenly spaced squares in alternating colors. The rules for matching even plaids also apply to large checks. However, checks that are ¼" wide or smaller or that are made of two close colors (black and gray, tan and medium brown) do not need to be matched. These fabrics take on the look of a solid or mottled when viewed in the quilt as a whole.

A more casual look is created by butting corner seams. Plaid butted corners do not need to be matched in any way. If a stripe is used along the length on the sides of a quilt, the top and bottom border strip stripes should be cut across the width.

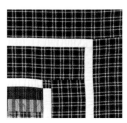

The stripes do not have to match at the butted seam and will still seem to flow from one border to the next.

Another alternative is to use corner squares. This eliminates difficult matching at the corners and avoids the awkward unmatched look.

Don't be afraid to try something new. Start out by adding just a bit of stripe or plaid as shown in Nosegay Stars and work up to larger amounts as used in Plaid Maze. Adding a stripe or plaid to your next quilt may be a change but will pay off in the end result. ∎

Antique Quilts

Early quiltmakers were not always concerned with matching stripes and plaids in their quilts. We will never know whether this was from the necessity to use every available piece of fabric or because they liked the effect of movement created with off-grain pieces.

Many old quilts with pieced blocks contain both plaids and stripes used with abandon. The grain may be aligned evenly with one edge of one piece and another edge of another piece in the same block, or with no edges at all. Sometimes the plaids and stripes were mixed with prints within a block. In other quilts, nothing but plaids and stripes were used in the pieced blocks that were then set with solid fabric squares. Both of these strategies use a non-plaid or -stripe to calm the crazy action of so many directionals.

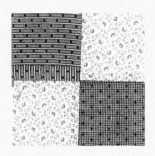

This antique block shows a pieced patch with no regard to fabric lines.

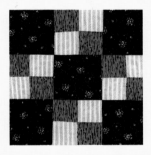

This block uses a stripe in a planned cutting arrangement.

This block uses a stripe that is placed haphazardly without regard to the stripe lines.

This antique quilt uses fine prints and white solid to offset the stripes.

Willy-Nilly

BY SANDRA L. HATCH

A variety of brushed flannel stripes and plaids combine in no specific order to make this easy-to-stitch quilt.

Project Notes

In this quilt, the plaids and stripes in the blocks are not fussy-cut. The strips were just cut as the name of the quilt implies, Willy-Nilly, or however they ended up.

The blue plaid fabric used on the border was a woven plaid. This means that the threads should be straight along the length and width of the fabric, allowing the lengthwise border strips to be fussy-cut.

A line was chosen on the fabric and fabric-length strips were cut along that line for all blue plaid border strips. When cutting strips in this manner, you must pay close attention when sewing to stitch along a line of the plaid as shown in Photo 1. If you miss stitching along the line, it is obvious as shown in Photo 2.

A Block
6" x 9" Block

B Block
9" x 9" Block

Photo 1

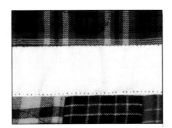

Photo 2

Project Specifications

Skill Level: Beginner
Quilt Size: 88" x 99"
Block Size: 6" x 9" and 9" x 9"
Number of Blocks: 56 and 16

Fabric & Batting

- 27 fat quarters assorted brushed flannel stripes and plaids
- 2½ yards cream solid
- 3 yards blue plaid
- Backing 94" x 105"
- Batting 94" x 105"

Supplies & Tools

- All-purpose thread to match fabrics
- Quilting thread
- Basic tools and supplies

Cutting

1. Cut six 2" by fabric width (20"–22") strips from the assorted 27 fat quarters or a total of 162 strips for A.

2. Cut three 6½" by fabric width strips cream solid; subcut strips into (63) 2" B strips.

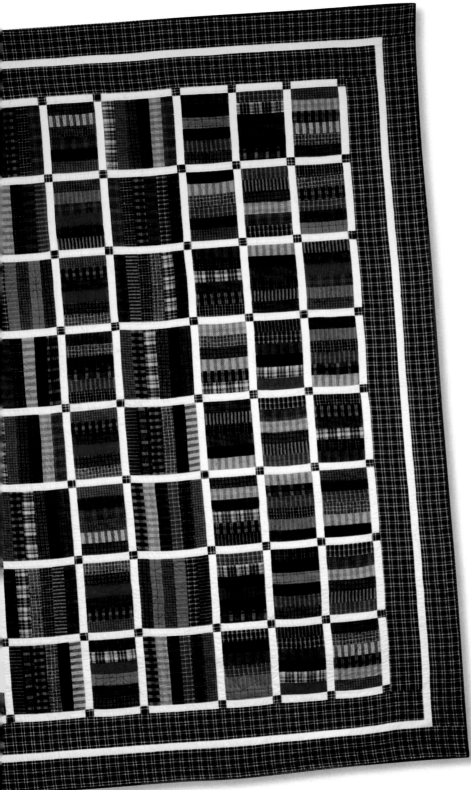

3. Cut five 9½" by fabric width strips cream solid; subcut strips into (98) 2" C strips.

4. Cut two 1½" strips along the length of the blue plaid; subcut into (90) 1½" D squares.

5. Cut two 4½" x 81½" E strips and two 4½" x 78½" F strips along length of blue plaid.

6. Cut nine 1½" by fabric width strips cream solid; join strips on short ends to make one long strip. Subcut strip into two 89½" G strips and two 80½" H strips.

7. Cut two 4 ½" x 91½" I strips and two 4½" x 88½" J strips along length of blue plaid.

8. Cut (21) 2¼" by 20"–22" strips assorted fat quarters for binding.

Piecing the Blocks

1. Select six different A strips; join with right sides together along length to make a strip set. Press seams in one direction; repeat for 27 strip sets.

2. Subcut strip sets into (56) 6½" A Blocks and (16) 9½" B Blocks as shown in Figure 1.

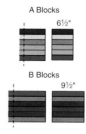

Figure 1
Subcut strip sets into
segments for blocks as shown.

Completing the Top

1. Join seven A Blocks with two B Blocks and 10 C strips to make a block row as shown in Figure 2; press seams toward blocks. Repeat for eight rows.

Figure 2
Make a block row as shown.

2. Join two C strips with seven B strips and 10 D squares to make a sashing row as shown in Figure 3; repeat for nine sashing rows. Press seams toward D squares.

Figure 3
Make a sashing row as shown.

3. Join the block rows and sashing rows to complete the pieced center; press seams toward block rows.

4. Sew an E strip to opposite long sides and an F strip to the top and bottom of the pieced center; press seams toward E and F.

5. Sew a G strip to opposite long sides and an H strip to the top and bottom of the pieced center; press seams toward G and H.

6. Sew an I strip to opposite long sides and a J strip to the top and bottom of the pieced center; press seams toward I and J.

Finishing the Quilt

1. Sandwich batting between the completed top and prepared backing; pin or baste to hold.

2. Quilt as desired by hand or machine.

3. When quilting is complete, remove pins or basting; trim batting and backing even with quilt top edges.

4. Join binding strips on short ends with a diagonal seam to make one long strip. Fold strip in half along length with wrong sides together to make a double-layered strip; press.

5. Stitch binding to quilt with the raw edges of the layered binding strip against the right side of the quilt top, mitering corners and overlapping at beginning and end. Turn binding to the wrong side; hand- or machine-stitch in place to finish. ■

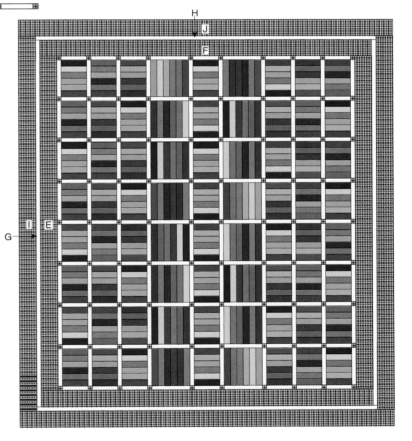

Willy-Nilly
Placement Diagram
88" x 99"

Plaid Maze

BY SANDRA L. HATCH

Stitch up a quilt in a day using plaids and stripes in quick-to-stitch blocks.

Project Notes

With some planning, you can miter both the plaid and striped corners on the borders of this easy quilt. Because this quilt is square, matching is simple.

Select and cut identical strips of the plaid and stripes for lines to come together at corners. Photo 1 shows the plaids matching at one border corner. Photo 2 shows the striped border miter. Note that the striped borders are the same on all corners. This was accomplished by selecting and cutting the striped strips a little longer than needed, then finding the center of the strip. If the same element of the stripe is centered on each side of the quilt when pinning in place, the corners will be a perfect match.

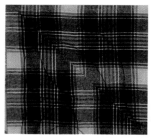

Photo 1

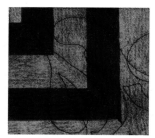

Photo 2

Project Specifications

Skill Level: Beginner
Quilt Size: 79" x 79"
Block Size: 14" x 14"
Number of Blocks: 16

Plaid Maze A
14" x 14" Block

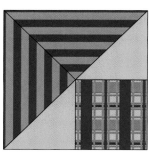

Plaid Maze B
14" x 14" Block

Fabric & Batting

- 1½ yards gold print
- 2⅝ yards blue 2-tone even-width stripe (sample uses dark and light blue ¾"-wide stripes)
- 3½ yards blue/gold plaid
- Backing 85" x 85"
- Batting 85" x 85"

Supplies & Tools

- All-purpose thread to match fabrics
- Quilting thread
- Basic tools and supplies

Cutting

1. Cut four 7½" by fabric width strips blue/gold plaid; subcut strips into (16) 7½" A squares.
***Note**: These strips may be identical if you plan for the A squares to be in the same position in each block. Note that in the sample quilt, the A squares are not identical.*

2. Cut two 7⅞" by fabric width strips gold print; subcut strips into eight 7⅞" squares. Cut each square in half to make 16 B triangles as shown in Figure 1.

Figure 1
Cut squares in half
to make B triangles.

Figure 2
Cut square in half on
both diagonals to make
C and D triangles.

3. Cut eight identical 15¼" x 15¼" squares blue 2-tone even-width stripe. Cut each square in half on both diagonals to make C and D triangles as shown in Figure 2.

4. Cut six 2½" by fabric width strips gold print. Join strips on short ends to make one long strip; subcut strip into two 56½" E strips and two 60½" F strips.

5. Cut seven identical 3½" by fabric width strips blue 2-tone even-width stripe. Join strips on short ends to make one long strip; subcut strip into four 70" G strips. **Note:** *These strips are longer than*

needed to facilitate matching plaid at mitered corners.

6. Cut four identical 7" strips from remaining fabric length blue/gold plaid. **Note**: *These strips are longer than needed to facilitate matching plaid at corners.*

7. Cut eight 2¼" by fabric width strips gold print for binding.

Piecing the Blocks

1. Sew B to two adjacent sides of A as shown in Figure 3; press seams toward B. Repeat for 16 A-B units.

Figure 3
Sew B to 2
adjacent sides of A.

2. Join two C triangles on short sides, matching stripe lines as shown in Figure 4; press seam to one side. Repeat for eight C units.

Figure 4
Join 2 C triangles on short
sides, matching stripe lines.

3. Sew a C unit to an A-B unit to complete one Plaid Maze A block as shown in Figure 5; press seams toward the C unit. Repeat for eight blocks.

Figure 5
Sew a C unit to an A-B
unit to complete 1 Plaid
Maze A block.

4. Join two D triangles on short sides, matching stripe lines as shown in Figure 6; press seam to one side. Repeat for eight D units.

Figure 6
Join 2 D triangles on
short sides, matching
stripe lines.

5. Sew a D unit to an A-B unit to complete one Plaid Maze B block as shown in Figure 7; press seams toward the D unit. Repeat for eight blocks.

Figure 7
Sew a D unit to an A-E
unit to complete 1
Plaid Maze B block.

Completing the Top

1. Join four Plaid Maze A blocks to make an A row as shown in Figure 8; press seams toward the C units. Repeat for two A rows.

Figure 8
Join 4 Plaid Maze A blocks
to make an A row.

2. Join four Plaid Maze B blocks to make a B row referring to Figure 9; press seams toward D units. Repeat for two B rows.

Figure 9
Join 4 Plaid Maze B blocks
to make a B row.

3. Join A and B rows, beginning with an A row and alternating rows referring to the Placement Diagram; press seams in one direction.

4. Sew an E strip to opposite sides and an F strip to the top and bottom of the pieced center; press seams toward E and F.

5. Fold one G strip to find the center. If the center is not in the center of one of the stripes, move fold to be in the center of one as shown in Figure 10; crease and place a pin to mark the center. Select the exact same stripe as the center of each of the remaining strips and mark.

Figure 10
Select the center of 1 stripe
for center of G strip.

6. Center a G strip on each side of the pieced center with excess at each end; pin in place and check that the stripes end at exactly the same place on each side of the pieced center. Adjust to make ends perfect, if necessary. Stitch each strip to a side, stopping stitching ¼" from each end. Miter each corner referring to Matching Stripes at Mitered Corners on page 62.

7. Repeat step 6 with H border strips to complete the pieced top.

Finishing the Quilt

1. Complete the quilt referring to Finishing the Quilt on page 9. ■

Plaid Maze
Placement Diagram
79" x 79"

Patriotic Bouquets

BY SANDRA L. HATCH

Using a stripe to simulate a strip-pieced triangle creates movement in this patriotic-looking quilt.

Cutting Striped Triangles

A striped fabric may be cut in triangle shapes to create the appearance of a strip-pieced triangle. The trick is to place the triangle template on the same exact location on the striped fabric for each triangle. This means paying strict attention to the printed lines on the stripe.

Select the lines on the stripe that you want to frame the center square. Photo 1 shows several stripes with different repeats.

Photo 1

Try to choose an area where the stitching line won't lie perfectly on a printed line as shown in Photo 2. It is not easy to use a line on the fabric as a guide for stitching, and unless your stitching is perfectly straight, another color(s) will often appear along the stitching line as shown in Photo 3.

The striped fabric used for the sample has a 6" repeat. Because the B triangle is 6⅝" high, the pieces cannot be butted across the fabric width for cutting. This creates waste between the striped areas needed for cutting as shown in Photo 4.

Photo 4

Because stripes are usually printed along the length of the fabric, it is easier to cut fabric-length strips. These strips are then cut into triangles using the B template given or the 45-degree-angle line on a rotary ruler as shown in Photos 5 and 6. The lengthwise waste sections between the stripe

Photo 5

Photo 2

Photo 3

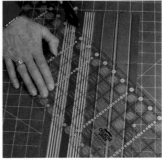

Photo 6

repeats may be fussy-cut for borders as shown in Photo 7.

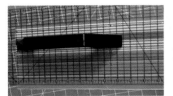 

Photo 7

When cutting the triangles from the strips, there is another same-size triangle leftover on the opposite side of the stripe as shown in Figure 1. These triangles may be set aside for another project.

Figure 1
Leftover triangles result from
cutting B triangles from strips.

The edges of the B triangles that will be placed on the outside edges of the block are bias edges. A line of stitching ⅛" from the edge of each short side of the triangles will stabilize the pieces, but even then, you must be careful not to stretch the edges during stitching. Another stabilizing alternative is a spray fabric stabilizer. This may be applied to the wrong side of the triangles after cutting. If you are very careful when handling the pieces, you don't need to worry about stretching.

Once the cutting process is finished, making the blocks and completing the top is quick and easy.

Project Specifications
Skill Level: Beginner
Quilt Size: 81" x 81"
Block Size: 17" x 17"
Number of Blocks: 9

Fabric & Batting
- 1⅛ yards blue print
- 1½ yards red print
- 3¼ yards floral/flag print
- 4½ yards red/white/blue stripe with 6" repeat
- Backing 87" x 87"
- Batting 87" x 87"

Patriotic Bouquet
17" x 17" Block

Supplies & Tools
- All-purpose thread to match fabrics
- Basic tools and supplies and ruler with a 45-degree-angle line (optional)

Cutting
1. Cut four 6½" by fabric width strips floral/flag print. Join strips on short ends to make one long strip. Cut two 69½" H strips from the strip.

2. Cut two 6½" x 81½" I strips along the remaining length of the floral/flag print.

3. Cut nine 12½" x 12½" squares on point along the length of the remaining floral/flag print referring to Figure 2.

Figure 2
Cut A squares along length of fabric as shown.

4. Select the area on the stripe for cutting B triangles referring to Cutting Striped Triangles. Cut 6⅝"-wide strips along the length of the red/white/blue stripe. **Note:** *The number of strips needed will vary depending on the chosen stripe. The striped repeat on the sample fabric was 6", which means there was waste between the lengthwise strips; this was used to cut the E border strips. The chosen fabric yielded three B strips from one width of fabric, which meant that 12 triangles were needed from each strip to yield 36 triangles. Each triangle is 13¼" long, so the strips needed to be cut 159" long (12 triangles times 13¼").*

5. Prepare template for B using pattern given and referring to Cutting Striped Triangles; cut 36 identical B triangles from the fabric-length strips. **Note:** *You may prefer to cut the triangles with a 45-degree-angle line on a ruler. Refer to Cutting Striped Triangles for instructions.*

6. Cut two 3½" by fabric width strips red print; subcut strips into (16) 3½" D squares.

7. Cut two 17½" by fabric width strips blue print; subcut strips into (24) 3½" C strips.

8. Select a striped area from the leftover red/white/blue stripe; cut four 1½" x 70" E strips, centering same-stripe area in each strip referring to Photos 2–7.

9. Cut seven 2½" by fabric width strips red print; join on short ends to make one long strip. Subcut strip into two 65½" F strips and two 69½" G strips.

10. Cut nine 2¼" by fabric width strips red print for binding.

Piecing the Blocks

1. Sew a B triangle to opposite sides of each A square to complete one block; press seams toward B. Repeat for nine blocks.

2. Square blocks to 17½" x 17½", if necessary.

Completing the Top

1. Join three blocks with four C strips to make a block row as shown in Figure 3; repeat for four rows. Press seams toward C. **Note**: *If your blocks are directional, be sure to keep them upright in the rows.*

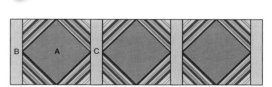

Figure 3
Join 3 blocks with 4 C sashing
strips to make a block row.

2. Join four D squares with three C strips to make a sashing row as shown in Figure 4; repeat for four sashing rows. Press seams toward C.

Figure 4
Join 4 D squares with 3 C sashing
strips to make a sashing row.

3. Join the block rows with the sashing rows to complete the pieced center; press seams toward sashing rows.

4. Center and sew an E strip to each side of the pieced center, mitering corners. Trim mitered seam to ¼"; press open. Press seams toward E. **Note**: *The stripe used for E is very narrow and requires precise matching at mitered corners referring to Matching Stripes at Mitered Corners on page 62.*

5. Sew an F strip to the top and bottom and a G strip to opposite long sides of the pieced center; press seams toward F and G.

6. Sew an H strip to the top and bottom and an I strip to opposite long sides of the pieced center; press seams toward H and I. **Note:** *If the fabrics are directional, be sure to keep the strips in an upright position when stitching to the pieced top.*

Finishing the Quilt
1. Complete the quilt referring to Finishing the Quilt on page 9. ■

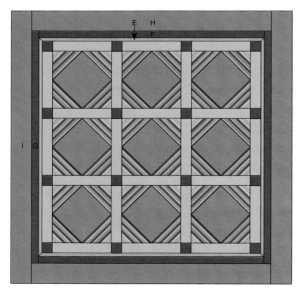

Patriotic Bouquets
Placement Diagram
81" x 81"

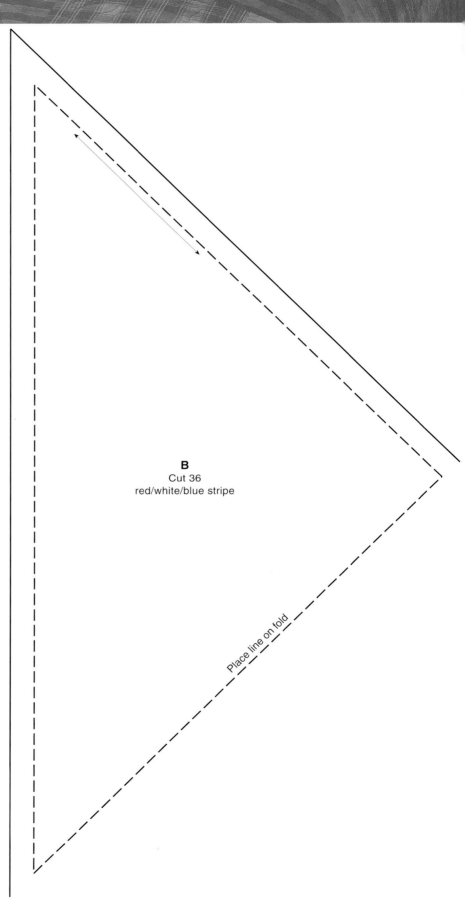

B
Cut 36
red/white/blue stripe

Place line on fold

Riding Around

BY SUE HARVEY

The subtle print/stripe fabrics in this quilt were used as prints with no attempt at matching direction or stripe lines.

Project Specifications
Skill Level: Intermediate
Quilt Size: 60" x 72"
Block Size: 12" x 12"
Number of Blocks: 12

Fabric & Batting
- ¾ yard blue/red plaid
- 1⅛ yards blue/cream stripe
- 1½ yards red print
- 1⅔ yards gold print
- 2½ yards blue print
- Backing 66" x 78"
- Batting 66" x 78"

Supplies & Tools
- All-purpose thread to match fabrics
- Quilting thread
- Basic tools and supplies

Cutting Pieces
1. Cut four strips blue print 3½" by width of fabric for L borders.

2. Cut two strips 3½" x 66½" along remaining length of blue print for K borders.

3. Cut two strips blue print 3⅞" by remaining width of fabric; subcut into (12) 3⅞" squares. Cut each square on one diagonal to make 24 D triangles.

4. Cut four F strips blue print 3½" by remaining width of fabric.

Railroad Crossing
12" x 12" Block

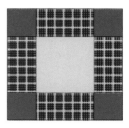

Counterpane
12" x 12" Block

5. Cut 10 strips blue print 3½" by remaining width of fabric; subcut into (94) 3½" H squares.

6. Cut four strips blue/cream stripe 4¾" by width of fabric; subcut two strips into (12) 4¾" B squares. Set aside remaining strips for A.

7. Cut one A strip gold print 4¾" by width of fabric.

8. Cut seven strips gold print 6½" by width of fabric; subcut six strips into (36) 6½" J squares. Set aside one strip for E.

9. Cut two strips red print 7¼" by width of fabric; subcut into (12) 7¼" squares. Cut each square on both diagonals to make 24 C triangles.

10. Cut nine strips red print 3½" by width of fabric; subcut three strips into seven 3½" x 12" G rectangles. Subcut the remaining strips into (72) 3½" H squares.

11. Cut two E strips blue/red plaid 3½" by width of fabric.

12. Cut two F strips blue/red plaid 6½" by width of fabric.

13. Cut seven strips blue/cream stripe 2¼" by width of fabric for binding.

Piecing Units

1. Sew the gold A strip between the two striped A strips along length with right sides together; press seams toward gold. Subcut into six 4¾" A units as shown in Figure 1.

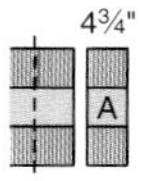

Figure 1
Cut the strip set into 4¾" A units.

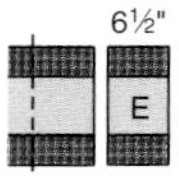

Figure 2
Cut the strip set into 6½" E units.

2. Sew the gold E strip between the two plaid E strips; press seams toward gold. Subcut into six 6½" E units as shown in Figure 2.

3. Sew a plaid F strip between two blue F strips; press seams toward blue. Repeat for two strip sets. Subcut into (19) 3½" F units as shown in Figure 3.

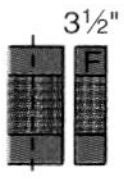

Figure 3
Cut the strip set into 3½" F units.

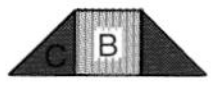

Figure 4
Complete a B-C unit.

4. Sew C to opposite sides of B to make a B-C unit as shown in Figure 4; repeat for 12 B-C units. Press seams toward C.

5. Draw a line from corner to corner on the wrong side of each H square.

6. Place a blue H right sides together on two corners of G as shown in Figure 5; stitch on the marked lines, trim seam allowances to ¼" and press H open as shown in Figure 6. Repeat for seven G-H units.

Figure 5
Place H on 2 corners of G.

Figure 6
Stitch, trim and press H open.

7. Place a blue H right sides together with a red H; stitch on marked line, trim and press open to make an H unit as shown in Figure 7; repeat for four H units.

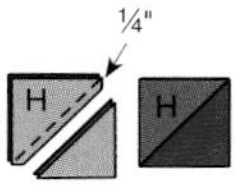

Figure 7
Complete an H unit.

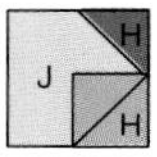

Figure 8
Place H on 2 adjacent corners of J.

8. Place a blue H on two adjacent corners of J as shown in Figure 8; stitch, trim and press open. Repeat with a red H on the remaining corners to make an H-J unit as shown in Figure 9. Repeat to make 32 H-J units.

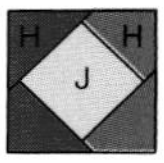

Figure 9
Complete an H-J unit.

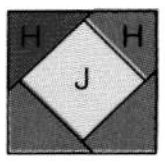

Figure 10
Complete a corner unit.

9. Place a blue H on three corners of J and a red H on the remaining corner; stitch, trim and press open to make a corner unit as shown in Figure 10. Repeat to make four corner units.

Piecing the Blocks and Borders

1. To piece one Railroad Crossing block, sew a B-C unit to opposite sides of an A as shown in

Figure 11; add D to each corner to complete one block. Repeat to make six blocks.

Figure 11
Complete 1 Railroad
Crossing block.

2. To piece one Counterpane block, sew an E unit between two F units to complete one block referring to the block drawing; repeat to make six blocks.

3. Sew a Counterpane block between two Railroad Crossing blocks to make a row; press seams toward Counterpane block. Repeat for two rows.

4. Sew a Railroad Crossing block between two Counterpane blocks to make a row; press seams toward Counterpane blocks. Repeat for two rows.

5. Join the rows to complete the center section referring to the Placement Diagram for positioning of rows; press seams in one direction.

6. Join two G-H units with two F units to make a side border strip as shown in Figure 12; press seams in one direction.

Figure 12
Complete a side border strip.

7. Sew a side border strip to opposite long sides of the center section referring to the Placement Diagram for positioning; press seams toward strips.

8. Join one G-H unit, two F units and two H units to make a top strip as shown in Figure 13; press. Sew the strip to the top of the center section referring to the Placement Diagram for positioning; press seam toward strip.

9. Join two G-H units, one F unit and two H units to make a bottom strip, again referring to Figure 13; press. Sew the strip to the bottom of the center section; press seam toward strip.

Figure 13
Complete 2 end border strips.

10. Join nine H-J units to make a strip, matching red to red and blue to blue; repeat. Sew a strip to opposite long sides of the center section referring to the Placement Diagram; press seams toward strips.

11. Join seven H-J units with two corner units to make a strip; repeat. Sew a strip to the top and bottom of the center section; press seams toward strips.

12. Sew a K strip to opposite long sides of the pieced center; press seams toward strips.

13. Join the L strips on short ends to make a long strip; press seams in one direction. Cut into two 60½" L strips.

14. Sew an L strip to the top and bottom of the pieced center to complete the top; press seams toward strips.

Finishing the Quilt

1. Complete the quilt referring to Finishing the Quilt on page 9. ■

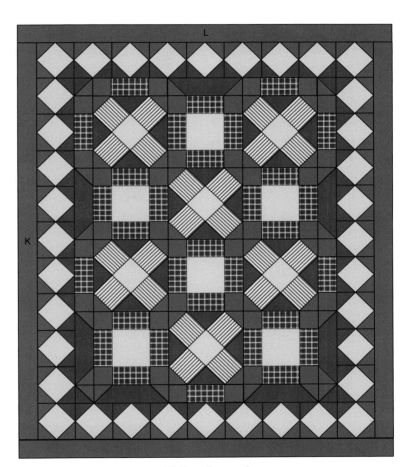

Riding Around
Placement Diagram
60" x 72"

Strips & Squares

BY SUE HARVEY

Use a large printed plaid as wide sashing strips and a bias cut of the same plaid for binding.

Project Specifications
Skill Level: Beginner
Quilt Size: 58½" x 69"
Block Size: 12¾" x 12¾"
Number of Blocks: 8

Fabric & Batting
- 1½ yards green flannel print
- 1¾ yards total assorted flannel prints
- 2⅝ yards large printed plaid flannel
- Backing 64" x 75"
- Batting 64" x 75"

Supplies & Tools
- Neutral color all-purpose thread
- Quilting thread
- Basic tools and supplies

Cutting
1. Cut four strips green print 7¼" by width of fabric; subcut into (16) 7¼" squares. Cut each square in half once diagonally to make 32 C triangles.

2. Cut six strips green print 3½" by width of fabric for E and F borders.

3. Cut three D strips 9½" x 51½" along length of large plaid, being careful to cut straight along edge of plaid lines as shown in the close-up photo.

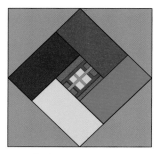

Strips & Square
12¾" x 12¾" Block

4. Cut eight 3½" A squares from remaining width of large plaid.

5. Cut two 18" by width of fabric strips from remaining length of large plaid. Cut into (11) 2½"-wide bias strips. **Note**: *Refer to instructions on page 60 for cutting bias strips.*

6. Cut (66) 3½" x 6½" B rectangles from assorted flannel prints.

7. Cut four 4¼" x 6½" G rectangles from assorted flannel prints.

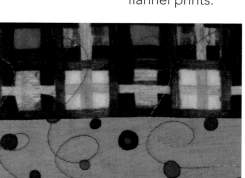

Piecing Blocks
1. Align a B rectangle with 2 edges of an A square as shown in Figure 1. Stitch, stopping 1" from the edge of the

Figure 1
Align B with 2 edges of A; stitch, stopping 1" from edge of A.

A square, again referring to Figure 1; backstitch. Press seam toward the B.

2. Align a second B rectangle along the stitched A-B edge; stitch along length of B as shown in Figure 2. Press seam toward B.

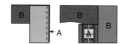

Figure 2
Stitch B to the A-B edge.

3. Add a third B rectangle to the A-B end referring to Figure 3; press seam toward B.

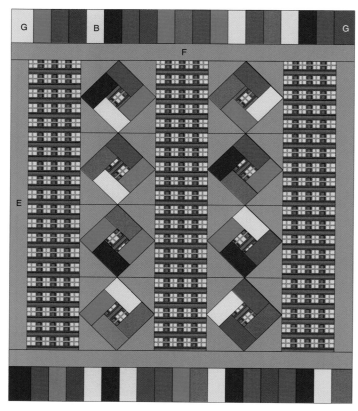

Strips & Squares
Placement Diagram
58½" x 69"

4. Fold back the end of the first B rectangle as shown in Figure 3. Align a fourth B rectangle along the remaining A-B edge and stitch in place, again referring to Figure 3; press seam toward B.

Figure 3
Fold back the B end;
stitch B to the A-B edge.

5. Align the unstitched edge of the first B rectangle along the edge of the A-B section and complete stitching of B as shown in Figure 4; press seam toward B.

Figure 4
Align the unstitched B
edge with the A-B unit;
complete stitching of B.

6. Center and stitch a C triangle to each edge of the A-B unit to complete one block as shown in Figure 5; press seams toward the C triangles.

Figure 5
Center and stitch C
to each edge of the
A-B unit to
complete 1 block.

7. Repeat steps 1–6 to complete eight blocks.

Completing the Top

1. Join four blocks to make a row as shown in Figure 6; press seams open between blocks. Repeat for two rows.

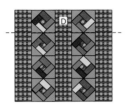

Figure 6
Join 4 blocks to make a row.

Figure 7
Align blocks across the center D strip.

2. Join the two block rows with the three D strips, aligning the top and bottom of each strip with the top and bottom of the block rows and checking to be sure that the blocks line up across the center D strip as shown in Figure 7. Press seams toward strips.

3. Join the E/F strips on short ends to make a long strip; press seams in one direction. Cut into two 51½" E strips and two 59" F strips.

4. Sew the E strips to opposite D edges of the pieced center and F to the top and bottom; press seams toward strips.

5. Join 17 B rectangles on long edges; press seams in one direction. Add a G rectangle to each end of the B strip; press seams toward G. Repeat for two pieced strips. Sew a strip to the top and bottom to complete the top; press seams toward F strips.

Finishing the Quilt

1. Complete the quilt referring to Finishing the Quilt on page 9 and Preparing Bias Strips on page 60. ∎

Cardinals Rule

BY SANDRA L. HATCH

A pretty cardinal print combines with a matching even-width stripe to keep your eye moving in this pretty bed-size quilt.

Project Notes

The cardinal print used in these blocks is directional. In order to keep them upright in each block, half the blocks are cut from top left to right bottom and the other half are cut from the right top to the left bottom as shown in Figure 1. If you are not using a directional print, it is not necessary to have both A and B blocks as is shown here.

Project Specifications

Skill Level: Beginner
Quilt Size: 93" x 93"
Block Size: 14½" x 14½"
Number of Blocks: 16

Fabric & Batting

- ⅔ yard brown print
- 1¼ yards green tonal
- 2 yards red mottled
- 2¼ yards red tonal stripe
- 4 yards cream print
- Backing 99" x 99"
- Batting 99" x 99"

Supplies & Tools

- All-purpose thread to match fabrics
- Quilting thread
- Basic tools and supplies

Cutting

1. Cut six 12⅞" by fabric width strips cream print; subcut strips into (16) 12⅞" squares. Cut each square on one diagonal to make 32 A triangles.

Cardinals Rule A
14½" x 14½" Block

Cardinals Rule B
14½" x 14½" Block

Note: *If using a directional fabric, cut eight squares each as shown in Figure 1 to keep design upright in blocks.*

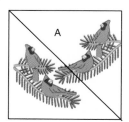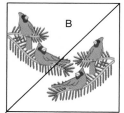

Figure 1
Cut squares on 1 diagonal as
shown if fabric is directional.

2. Cut two 22" by fabric width strips red tonal stripe; subcut strips into (16) 4⅛" B rectangles, centering the same part of the stripe in each strip as shown in Figure 2.

Figure 2
Cut 4⅛" B rectangles, centering the same
part of the stripe in each strip as shown.

3. Cut two 15" by fabric width strips green tonal; subcut strips into (40) 2" C strips.

4. Cut three 15" by fabric width strips red mottled; subcut strips into (80) 1¼" D strips.

5. Cut two 3½" by fabric width strips brown print; subcut strips into (24) 3½" E squares. Cut one more 3½" x 3½" E square from brown print for a total of 25 E squares.

6. Cut eight 1" by fabric width strips green tonal; join strips on short ends, trim seam to ¼" and press open to reduce bulk as shown in Figure 3 to make one long strip. Subcut strip into four 73½" F strips.

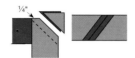

Figure 3
Join strips as shown; trim seam to
¼" and press open to reduce bulk.

7. Cut eight 1½" by fabric width strips brown print; join strips on short ends to make one long strip. Subcut strip into two 73½" G strips and two 75½" H strips.

8. Cut eight 3½" by fabric width strips red tonal stripe; join strips on short ends to make one long strip, sewing pieces together to continue stripe pattern as shown in Figure 4. Subcut strips into two 75½" I strips and two 81½" J strips.

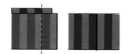

Figure 4
Join strips to continue
striped pattern.

9. Cut nine 6½" by fabric width strips cream print; join strips on short ends to make one long strip. Subcut strip into two 81½" K strips and two 93½" L strips. **Note**: If using a directional print, cut five 6½" by fabric width strips and join on short ends to make L strips, and cut and piece two 6½" x 81½" strips along the length to make K strips.

10. Cut (10) 2¼" by fabric width strips red mottled for binding.

Piecing the Blocks

1. Fold and crease two A triangles to find the center of the longest or diagonal side; mark with a pin. Note: If using a directional print, be sure to select two A triangles that will finish in an upright position referring to Figure 1.

2. Fold a B strip across width to find the center; mark with a pin.

3. Sew a B strip between two A triangles, matching pinned centers as shown in Figure 5; stitch. Press seams toward A.

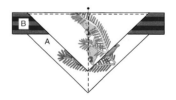

Figure 5
Sew a B strip between 2 A triangles,
matching pinned centers.

4. Trim excess B at corners to make square as shown in Figure 6; trim block to 15" if necessary to complete one block. Repeat for 16 blocks. **Note**: If using a directional print, repeat for eight each A and B blocks referring to the block drawings.

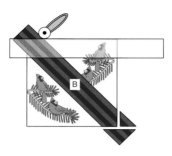

Figure 6
Trim excess B at corners.

Completing the Top

1. Sew a D strip to each side of C as shown in Figure 7; press seams toward D. Repeat for 40 C-D sashing units.

Figure 7
Sew a D strip to each side of C.

2. Join five sashing units with four blocks to complete a block row as shown in Figure 8; press seams toward sashing units. Repeat for four rows. *Note: If using a directional print, you will need two A block rows and two B block rows, again referring to Figure 8.*

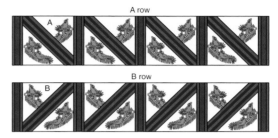

Figure 8
Join 5 sashing units with 4 blocks to complete a block row. If using a directional print, you will need A and B block rows.

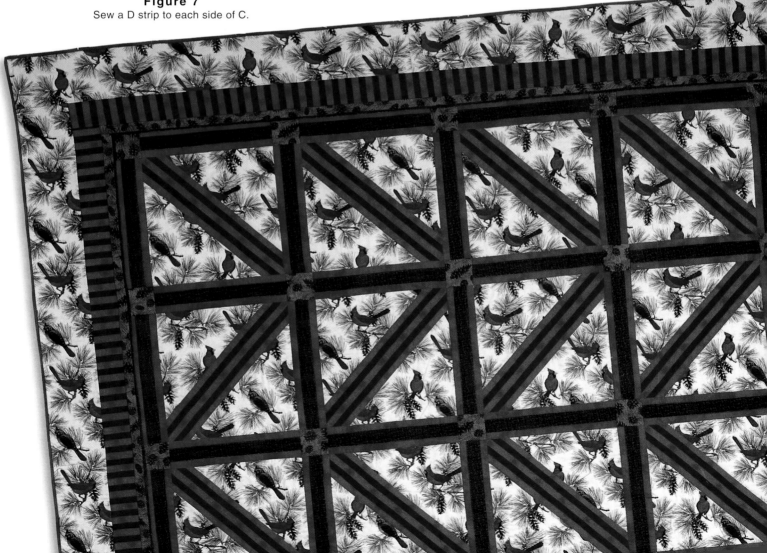

3. Join four sashing units with five E squares to make a sashing row as shown in Figure 9; press seams toward sashing units. Repeat for five sashing rows.

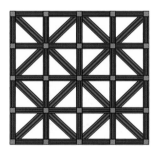

Figure 9
Join 4 sashing units with 5 E squares to make a sashing row.

4. Join the block rows with the sashing rows referring to the Placement Diagram to complete the pieced center; press seams toward sashing rows. **Note:** *Figure 10 shows an alternate placement of the blocks to create a different design where the B pieces come together.*

Figure 10
If the blocks are joined with the B pieces coming together, the design takes on a new look.

5. Press each F strip in half with wrong sides together along length to make a double-layered strip.

6. Pin an F strip to opposite sides of the pieced center with raw edges even; stitch in place. Repeat with F strips on the top and bottom of the pieced center. **Note**: *The F strips do not add any size to the pieced top; instead, they provide a color break between the pieced center and the first border strips.*

7. Sew a G strip to opposite sides and an H strip to the top and bottom of the pieced center; press seams toward G and H.

8. Sew an I strip to opposite sides and a J strip to the top and bottom of the pieced center; press seams toward I and J.

9. Sew a K strip to opposite sides and an L strip to the top and bottom of the pieced center; press seams toward K and L.

Finishing the Quilt
1. Complete the quilt referring to Finishing the Quilt on page 9. ■

Cardinals Rule
Placement Diagram
93" x 93"

Flower Paths

BY SUE HARVEY

A printed plaid is cut with edges of pieces aligned with the plaid lines for the blocks and without regard to the plaid lines for the border in this twin-size quilt.

Project Specifications
Skill Level: Intermediate
Quilt Size: 66" x 80"
Block Size: 14" x 14"
Number of Blocks: 12

Fabric & Batting
- 1¼ yards cream print
- 1⅝ yards gold weave
- 1⅔ yards burgundy mottled
- 2 yards printed plaid
- 2⅛ yards floral
- Backing 72" x 86"
- Batting 72" x 86"

Supplies & Tools
- Neutral color all-purpose thread
- Quilting thread
- Basic tools and supplies

Cutting
1. Cut two strips each 6½" x 66½" (R) and 6½" x 68½" (Q) along length of floral.

2. Cut six 6½" A squares from remaining width of floral.

3. Cut three strips gold weave 6½" by width of fabric; subcut into (24) 4½" x 6½" B rectangles.

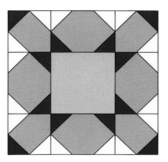

Nine-Patch Flower
14" x 14" Block

Checkerboard Corners
14" x 14" Block

4. Cut three strips gold weave 4½" by width of fabric; subcut into (24) 4½" C squares.

5. Cut seven strips gold weave 2¼" by width of fabric for binding.

6. Cut two strips cream print 2½" by width of fabric for G.

7. Cut nine strips cream print 2½" by width of fabric; subcut strips into (96) 2½" D squares and (24) 2½" F squares. Draw a diagonal line from corner to corner on the wrong side of each D square.

8. Cut five strips cream print 2½" by width of fabric for J and K borders.

9. Cut two strips burgundy mottled 2½" by width of fabric for G.

10. Cut 10 strips burgundy mottled 2½" by width of fabric; subcut strips into (148) 2½" E squares. Draw a diagonal line from corner to corner on the wrong side of each square.

11. Cut three strips burgundy mottled 2⅞" by width of fabric; subcut strips into (36) 2⅞" squares. Cut each square on one diagonal to make 72 H triangles.

12. Cut six strips burgundy mottled 2½" by width of fabric for L and M borders.

13. Cut six 14½" I squares from printed plaid, being careful to align edge of square with a line in the plaid.

14. Cut three strips printed plaid 6½" by width of fabric; subcut strips into (34) 2½" x 6½" N rectangles.

15. Cut one strip printed plaid 2½" by width of fabric; subcut into four 2½" x 4½" O rectangles and two 2½" x 8½" P rectangles.

Piecing Nine-Patch Flower Blocks

1. Place an E square right sides together on one corner of B; stitch on the marked line, trim seam allowance to ¼" and press E to the right side as shown in Figure 1.

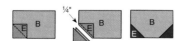

Figure 1
Place E on 1 corner of B; stitch, trim and press. Repeat on an adjacent corner of B.

2. Repeat on an adjacent corner of B, again referring to Figure 1.

3. Repeat steps 1 and 2 with two D square on the B-E unit to complete one B-D-E unit as shown in Figure 2; repeat to complete 24 B-D-E units.

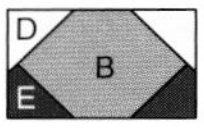

Figure 2
Complete 1
B-D-E unit.

Figure 3
Complete 1
C-D-E unit.

4. Repeat step 1 on the two D squares and one E square on C to complete a C-D-E unit as shown in Figure 3; repeat to complete 24 C-D-E units.

5. Sew a B-D-E unit to opposite sides of A to make a row as shown in Figure 4; press seams toward A.

6. Sew a C-D-E unit to opposite ends of a B-D-E unit to make a row, again referring to Figure 4; press seams toward the C-D-E units. Repeat.

7. Join the rows to complete one Nine-Patch Flower block; press seams away from the center row. Repeat to make six blocks.

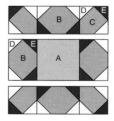

Figure 4
Join the units
with A in rows.

Piecing Checkerboard Corners Blocks

1. Sew a cream print G strip to a burgundy

mottled G strip; press seams toward burgundy mottled. Repeat for two strip sets.

2. Cut the strip sets into (24) 2½" G segments as shown in Figure 5.

Figure 5
Cut strip sets into 2½" G segments.

Figure 6
Complete 1 corner unit.

3. Sew an H triangle to the cream end of each G segment as shown in Figure 6; press seam toward H.

4. Sew an H triangle to each F square, again referring to Figure 6; press seam toward H.

5. Join a G-H unit and F-H unit with an H triangle to complete one corner unit, again referring to Figure 6; press seams in one direction. Repeat to make 24 corner units.

6. Measure 6⅛" from corner on each side of the I squares and make a mark as shown in Figure 7; place a ruler from mark to mark at one corner and trim off corner, again referring to Figure 7. Repeat on each corner of each I square.

Figure 7
Trim corners of I.

Figure 8
Complete 1 Checkerboard Corners block.

7. Sew a corner unit to each corner of the trimmed I square to complete one Checkerboard Corners block as shown in Figure 8; press seams toward I. Repeat to make six blocks.

Completing the Top
1. Sew a Checkerboard Corners block between two Nine-Patch Flowers blocks to make a row; press seams toward the Checkerboard Corners block. Repeat for two rows.

2. Sew a Nine-Patch Flowers block between two Checkerboard Corners blocks to make a row; press seams toward the Checkerboard Corners blocks. Repeat for two rows.

3. Join the rows to complete the pieced center referring to the Placement Diagram for positioning of rows; press seams open between rows.

4. Join the J/K border strips on short ends to make a long strip; press seams in one direction. Cut the strip into two 56½" J strips and two 46½" K strips.

5. Sew J to opposite long sides and K to the top and bottom of the pieced center; press seams toward strips.

6. Join the L/M border strips on short ends to make a long strip; press seams in one direction. Cut the strip into two 60½" L strips and two 50½" M strips.

7. Sew L to opposite long sides and M to the top and bottom of the pieced center; press seams toward strips.

8. Repeat step 1 of Piecing Nine-Patch Flower Blocks to complete 34 E-N units and two each E-P, E-O and E-O reversed units as shown in Figure 9.

Make 34
Make 2
Make 2 Make 2

Figure 9
Complete units as shown.

9. Join eight E-N units with one E-P unit, one E-O unit and one E-O reversed unit to make a side border strip as shown in Figure 10; press seams in one direction. Repeat for two strips.

E-O   E-N   E-P   E-O reversed

Figure 10
Join units to make a side border strip.

10. Referring to the Placement Diagram, sew a side border strip to opposite long sides of the pieced center; press seams toward the L strips.

11. Join nine E-N units to make a strip as shown in Figure 11; press seams in one direction. Repeat for two strips.

E-N

Figure 11
Join 9 E-N units to make a strip.

12. Referring to the Placement Diagram, sew an E-N strip to the top and bottom of the pieced center; press seams toward the M strips.

13. Sew the Q strips to opposite long sides and the R strips to the top and bottom of the pieced center to complete the top; press seams toward strips.

Finishing the Quilt

1. Complete the quilt referring to Finishing the Quilt on page 9. ■

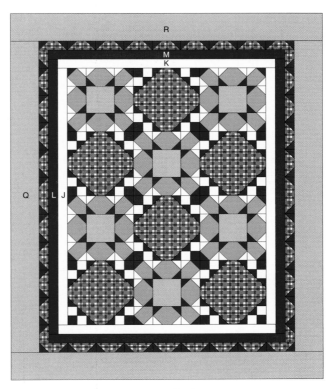

Flower Paths
Placement Diagram
66" x 80"

Nosegay Stars

BY SANDRA L. HATCH

Beautiful fabrics blend in the three block combinations used in this pretty quilt.

Project Notes

The A squares in the Nosegay blocks were fussy-cut from the red/violet floral. This is easy to accomplish using a clear template cut 4½" x 4½" square. Mark the center of the template with a dot and center the dot on a floral motif in the fabric as shown in Photo 1.

Photo 1

The striped G squares used in the center of the Stripe Star blocks were cut on point on the same position on the stripe so that when joined the stripe creates diagonal squares in the center of the blocks as shown in Photo 2.

Photo 2

To cut identical G squares, cut a 2½" x 2½" clear template. Place the template on the stripe on point as shown in Photo 3 to determine the area of the stripe to be used for each piece. When this decision is made, draw lines on the template to match with the stripe as shown in Photo 4. When using the template to cut pieces, align the drawn lines with the lines on the stripe to create identical pieces.

Photo 3

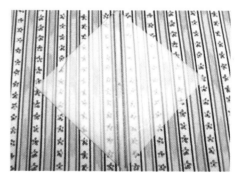

Photo 4

The G squares will have bias edges on all sides. To help keep these squares from stretching, a spray fabric stabilizer was applied to the wrong side of each square after cutting.

Project Specifications
Skill Level: Advanced
Quilt Size: 70" x 86"
Block Size: 8" x 8"
Number of Blocks: 39

Fabric & Batting
- ⅓ yard white floral
- ⅝ yard coordinating stripe
- ⅞ yard each yellow and purple prints
- 1⅔ yards cream tonal
- 1⅞ yards red/violet tonal
- 2½ yards red/violet floral
- Backing 76" x 92"
- Batting 76" x 92"

Supplies & Tools
- All-purpose thread to match fabrics
- Quilting thread
- Spray fabric stabilizer
- Basic tools and supplies and see-thru template material

Cutting
1. Center and fussy-cut (17) 4½" x 4½" floral motifs from the red/violet floral for A, referring to Photo 1 on page 38.

2. Cut (10) 2½" by fabric width strips each purple (B) and yellow (C) prints.

3. Cut (12) 2⅞" by fabric width strips each cream (D) and red/violet (E) tonals; subcut strips into (160) 2⅞" squares each D and E. Mark a line from corner to corner on the wrong side of each D square.

4. Cut eight 2½" by fabric width strips cream tonal; subcut strips into (116) 2½" F squares.

5. Prepare a 2½" x 2½" clear template for G. *Note*: Refer to the Project Notes and Photos

Stripe Star
8" x 8" Block

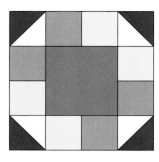

Nosegay
8" x 8" Block

Flower Star
8" x 8" Block

2–4 on page 38 to prepare template and cut G pieces. Cut five 3½" by fabric width strips from coordinating stripe. Fussy-cut 64 identical G squares on point.

6. Cut six 4½" x 4½" H squares white floral.

7. Cut (10) 2½" x 4½" I rectangles white floral.

8. Cut one 4½" by fabric width strip red/violet floral; subcut strip into (14) 2½" J rectangles.

9. Cut six 1½" by fabric width strips red/violet tonal; join strips on short ends to make one long strip. Subcut strip into two 64½" K strips and two 50½" L strips.

10. Cut seven 8½" by fabric width strips red/violet floral; join strips on short ends to make one long strip. Subcut strip into two 70½" M strips and two 54½" N strips.

HOUSE OF WHITE BIRCHES, BERNE, INDIANA 46711 WWW.WHITEBIRCHES.COM

11. Cut eight 2¼" by fabric width strips red/violet tonal for binding.

Piecing the Units

1. Place a D square right sides together with an E square. Referring to Figure 1, sew ¼" on each side of the drawn line. Cut apart on the drawn line and press seams toward E to complete two D-E units. Repeat to make 320 D-E units.

Figure 1
Complete D-E units as shown.

2. Sew a B strip to a C strip to make a strip set; repeat for nine strip sets. Press seams toward B strips. Subcut strip sets into (140) 2½" B-C units. Subcut the remaining B and C strips into (16) 2½" B and C squares. Set aside 58 B-C units and two each B and C squares for borders.

Piecing Nosegay Blocks

1. To complete one Nosegay block, sew a B-C unit to opposite sides of A as shown in Figure 2; press seams toward B-C.

Figure 2
Sew a B-C unit to opposite sides of A.

2. Sew a D-E unit to each end of a B-C unit as shown in Figure 3; press seams toward B-C units. Repeat for two B-C-D-E units.

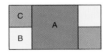

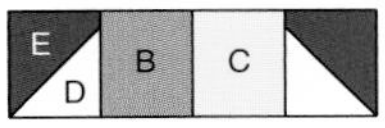

Figure 3
Sew a D-E unit to each end of a B-C unit.

3. Sew a B-C-D-E unit to opposite sides of the A-B-C unit as shown in Figure 4 to complete one Nosegay block; press seams toward the B-C-D-E units. Repeat for 17 blocks.

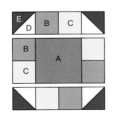

Figure 4
Sew a B-C-D-E unit to opposite sides of the A-B-C unit.

Piecing Stripe Star Blocks

1. To complete one Stripe Star block, join four G squares, matching stripes to complete a G center unit as shown in Figure 5.

Figure 5
Join 4 G squares, matching stripes to complete a G center unit.

2. Join two D-E units as shown in Figure 6; repeat for four units. Press seams in one direction.

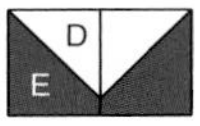

Figure 6
Join 2 D-E units.

Figure 7
Sew a D-E unit to opposite sides of the G center unit.

3. Sew a D-E unit to opposites sides of the G center unit as shown in Figure 7; press seams toward G.

4. Sew an F square to opposite ends of each remaining D-E unit; press seams toward F.

5. Sew a D-E-F unit to opposite sides of the D-E-G unit as shown in Figure 8 to complete one Stripe Star block; press seams toward D-E-F units. Repeat for 16 blocks.

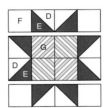

Figure 8
Sew a D-E-F unit to opposite sides of the D-E-G unit.

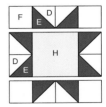

Figure 9
Join pieced units with H to complete 1 block.

Piecing Flower Star Blocks

1. Repeat steps 2–5 of Piecing Stripe Star Blocks replacing G with H in the center to complete one Flower Star block as shown in Figure 9; repeat for six blocks.

Piecing End and Corner Units

1. Join two D-E units with I as shown in Figure 10; press seams toward I. Repeat for 10 D-E-I units.

2. Join two D-E units with 2 F squares as shown in Figure 11; press seams toward F. Repeat for 10 D-E-F units.

Figure 10
Join 2 D-E units with I.

Figure 11
Join 2 D-E units
with 2 F squares.

3. Join one D-E-I unit with one D-E-F unit to complete one I end unit as shown in Figure 12; press seams toward D-E-I units. Repeat for 10 I end units.

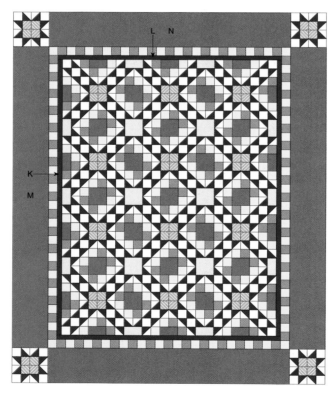

Nosegay Stars
Placement Diagram
70" x 86"

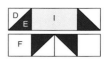

Figure 12
Join 1 D-E-I unit with
1 D-E-F unit to
complete an I unit.

Figure 13
Sew B and C to J.

4. Sew B and C to J as shown in Figure 13; press seams toward B and C. Repeat for 14 B-C-J units.

5. Sew a D-E unit to each end of a B-C unit as shown in Figure 14; press seams toward B-C unit. Repeat for 14 B-C-D-E units.

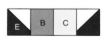

Figure 14
Sew a D-E unit to each
end of a B-C unit.

Figure 15
Join a B-C-J unit
with a B-C-D-E
unit to complete
1 J end unit.

6. Join a B-C-J unit with a B-C-D-E unit to complete one J end unit as shown in Figure 15; press seams toward B-C-J units. Repeat for 14 J end units.

7. Sew F to a D-E unit as shown in Figure 16; press seam toward F. Repeat for eight units.

Figure 16
Sew F to a D-E unit.

Figure 17
Join 2 D-E-F units to
complete a corner unit.

8. Join two D-E-F units to complete a corner unit as shown in Figure 17; press seams in one direction. Repeat for four corner units.

Completing the Top

1. Join two corner units with two I and three J end units to make the top row as shown in Figure 18; press seams toward I units. Repeat for bottom row.

Figure 18
Join 2 corner units with 2 I and 3 J end units to make the top row.

2. Join two J end units with two Nosegay blocks and three Stripe Star blocks to make a row as shown in Figure 19; press seams toward Nosegay blocks. Repeat for four rows.

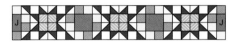

Figure 19
Join 2 J end units with 2 Nosegay blocks and 3 Stripe Star blocks to make a row.

3. Join two I end units with two Flower Star blocks and three Nosegay blocks to make a row as shown in Figure 20; press seams toward Nosegay blocks and I units. Repeat for three rows.

Figure 20
Join 2 I end units with 2 Flower Star blocks and 3 Nosegay blocks to make a row.

4. Join the block rows, beginning with J end unit rows and alternating with I end unit rows; add the top and bottom rows to complete the pieced center; press seams in one direction.

5. Sew a K strip to opposite long sides and an L strip to the top and bottom of the pieced center; press seams toward K and L.

6. Join 16 B-C units to make a long strip; add a B

square to one end. Press seams toward B squares; repeat for two strips. Sew a strip to opposite sides of the pieced center; press seams toward K strips.

7. Repeat step 6 with 13 B-C units, adding a C square to one end of each strip. Sew the strips to the top and bottom of the pieced center; press seams toward L strips.

8. Sew an M strip to opposite long sides of the pieced center; press seams toward M.

9. Sew a Stripe Star block to each end of each N strip; press seams toward N.

10. Sew a block/N strip to the top and bottom of the pieced center to complete the pieced top; press seams toward block/N strips.

Finishing the Quilt

1. Complete the quilt referring to Finishing the Quilt on page 9. ■

Starring Stripes

BY SUE HARVEY

Use a stripe to add interest to a simple pieced design.

Project Specifications
Skill Level: Beginner
Quilt Size: 70" x 88"
Block Size: 16" x 16"
Number of Blocks: 12

Fabric & Batting
- 1 yard each 6 stripe fabrics
- 5⅓ yards black mottled
- Backing 76" x 94"
- Batting 76" x 94"

Supplies & Tools
- Black all-purpose thread
- Quilting thread
- Basic tools and supplies and acrylic square with diagonal line

Cutting
1. Cut two 8½" x 8½" A squares from each striped fabric.

2. Cut two strips 4½" by width of fabric from each striped fabric; subcut into (16) 4½" B squares of each stripe. Draw a diagonal line from corner to corner on the wrong side of each square.

3. Cut one 15" by width of fabric strip from each striped fabric. Cut into (11) 2¼" x 21" bias strips total for binding. Cut one strip black mottled 7½" by width of fabric; cut into (10) 2¼" x 10½" bias strips **Note:** *Refer to instructions on page 62 for cutting bias strips.*

4. Cut 11 strips black mottled 4½" by width of fabric; subcut into (96) 4½" C squares. Draw a diagonal line from corner to corner on the wrong side of each square.

5. Cut six strips black mottled 8½" by width of fabric; subcut into (48) 4½" x 8½" D rectangles.

6. Cut four strips black mottled 2½" by width of fabric; subcut into eight 16½" E strips.

7. Cut nine strips black mottled 2½" by width of fabric for F, G and H.

8. Cut two strips black mottled 3½" by width of fabric; subcut into two 14½" I strips and two 8½" J strips.

9. Cut eight strips black mottled 4½" by width of fabric for K and L.

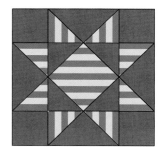

Variable Star
16" x 16" Block

Piecing Variable Star Blocks
1. Place a C square right sides together on one corner of an A square; stitch on the marked line, trim seam allowance to ¼" and press C to the right side as shown in Figure 1. Repeat on each corner of A to complete

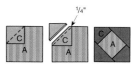

Figure 1
Complete an A-C unit.

one A-C unit, again referring to Figure 1. Repeat with all A squares. **Note:** *Leave trimmed-off triangles layered in pairs with edges aligned and set aside for the pieced border.*

2. Place a B square right sides together on one end of D referring to Figure 2 for correct placement of the B square stripes; stitch on the marked line, trim seam allowance to ¼" and press B to the right side, again referring to Figure 2. Repeat on the remaining end of D to complete one B-D unit, again referring to Figure 2. Repeat with all D rectangles. **Note:** *Leave trimmed-off triangles layered in pairs with edges aligned and set aside for the pieced border.*

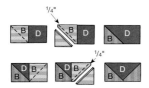

Figure 2
Complete a B-D unit.

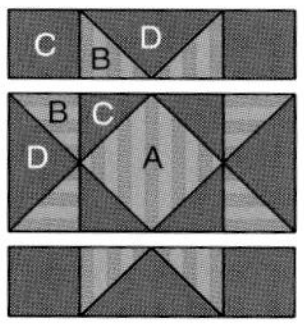

Figure 3
Join units
in rows.

3. Using same-stripe fabric units to complete one block, sew B-D to opposite sides of A-C to complete the block center row as shown in Figure 3; press seams toward A-C.

4. Sew a C square to opposite ends of B-D, again referring to Figure 3; press seams toward C. Repeat for two rows.

5. Join the rows to complete one Variable Star block; press seams away from the center row. Repeat to make two blocks of each striped fabric.

Completing the Top
1. Join three blocks with two E strips to make a block row as shown in Figure 4; press seams toward E. Repeat for four rows referring to the Placement Diagram for positioning of stripe colors.

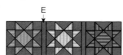

Figure 4
Join 3 blocks with 2 E strips.

2. Join the F/G/H strips on short ends to make a long strip; press seams in one direction. Cut into three 52½" F strips, two 70½" G strips and two 56½" H strips.

3. Join the block rows with the F strips to complete the pieced center; press seams toward F.

4. Sew G to opposite long sides and H to the top and bottom of the pieced center; press seams toward strips.

5. Stitch a layered triangle pair along the diagonal to make an X square as shown in Figure 5; press seam toward the black triangle. Repeat to make six X squares of four striped fabrics and seven X squares of two striped fabrics.

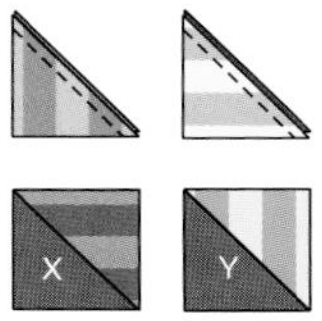

Figure 5
Sew layered triangles to
make X and Y squares

6. Stitch a layered triangle pair along the diagonal to make a Y square, again referring to Figure 5; press seam toward the black triangle. Repeat to make six Y squares of four striped fabrics and seven Y squares of two striped fabrics.

7. Place the diagonal line of the acrylic square over the seam of an X square and align two adjacent edges of the square with the 3½" lines of the ruler as shown in Figure 6; trim excess from remaining two sides to result in a 3½" square. Repeat with all X and Y squares.

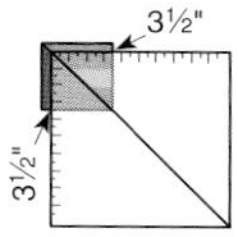

Figure 6
Trim X and Y
squares to 3½".

8. Join one each same-stripe X and Y squares to make an X-Y unit as shown in Figure 7; press seam to one side. Repeat to make six units of each stripe. **Note:** *The four extra pieced squares will be used in the corners of the pieced border.*

Figure 7
Complete an
X-Y unit.

9. Join 10 X-Y units with I to make a side border strip as shown in Figure 8; press seams in one direction between X-Y units and toward I. Repeat for two side border strips referring to the Placement Diagram for positioning of stripe colors.

Figure 8
Complete a side border strip.

10. Sew a side border strip to opposite long sides of the pieced center referring to the Placement Diagram for positioning of strips; press seams toward the G strips.

11. Join eight X-Y units with J and add an X or Y square to each end to make an end border strip as shown in Figure 9; press seams in one direction between units and toward J and the X and Y squares. Repeat for two end border strips referring to the Placement Diagram for positioning of stripe colors.

Figure 9
Complete an end border strip.

12. Sew an end border strip to the top and bottom of the pieced center referring to the Placement Diagram for positioning of strips; press seams toward the H strips.

13. Join the K/L strips on short ends to make a long strip; press seams in one direction. Cut into two 80½" K strips and two 70½" L strips.

14. Sew K to opposite long sides and L to the top and bottom of the pieced center to complete the top; press seams toward strips.

Finishing the Quilt

1. Join the binding strips to make a long strip, beginning with a black strip and alternating stripe colors with the black strips as shown in Figure 10 and referring to instructions on page 60; press seams toward the black strips.

Figure 10
Join binding strips with a diagonal seam; alternate black with stripe colors.

2. Press the strip in half along length with wrong sides together.

3. Complete the quilt referring to Finishing the Quilt on page 9. ■

Starring Stripes
Placement Diagram
70" x 88"

Framed in Plaid Flowers

BY SUE HARVEY

Versatile plaids work as well for appliqué as they do for piecing.

Project Specifications
Skill Level: Intermediate
Quilt Size: 54" x 66"
Block Size: 6" x 6"
Number of Blocks: 20

Fabric & Batting
- 1 fat quarter each 8 plaids
- ¾ yard olive/red plaid
- ¾ yard cream plaid
- 1 yard olive print
- 1⅛ yards tan print
- 1⅓ yards red texture
- Backing 60" x 72"
- Batting 60" x 72"

Supplies & Tools
- Tan and black all-purpose thread
- Quilting thread
- ¾ yard 12"-wide light double-stick fusible web
- Basting glue with applicator tip
- Basic tools and supplies

Cutting
1. Cut seven strips tan print 3½" by width of fabric; subcut into (76) 3½" A squares.

2. Cut four strips tan print 2" by width of fabric for B.

Four-Patch
6" x 6" Block

Double Four-Patch
6" x 6" Block

3. Cut four strips red texture 2" by width of fabric for C.

4. Cut four strips red texture 1¼" by width of fabric; subcut into two 36½" E strips, two 26" F strips and eight 3½" M strips.

5. Cut two L strips 1¼" x 41" red texture.

6. Cut eight strips red texture 1¼" by width of fabric for K, N and O.

7. Cut six strips red texture 2¼" by width of fabric for binding.

8. Cut four strips olive print 2¾" by width of fabric; subcut into two 38" G strips and two 30½" H strips.

9. Cut six strips olive print 3½" by width of fabric for P and Q.

10. Cut four strips cream plaid 5" by width of fabric; subcut into two 42½" I strips and two 39½" J strips.

11. Cut six 3½" x 3½" D squares from each plaid fat quarter and olive/red plaid.

12. Cut one strip olive/red plaid 18" by width of fabric; cut eight ⅜" x 25" bias strips. **Note:** *Refer to instructions on page 60 for cutting bias strips.*

Piecing Four-Patch Blocks

1. Sew an A square to a D square as shown in Figure 1; press seams toward D. Repeat for 48 A-D units.

Figure 1
Sew A to D.

Figure 2
Complete 1
Four-Patch block.

2. Join two A-D units to complete one Four-Patch block as shown in Figure 2; press seam to one side. Repeat for eight blocks. Set aside remaining A-D units.

Piecing Double Four-Patch Blocks

1. Sew a B strip to a C strip with right sides together along length; press seam toward C. Repeat for four strip sets.

2. Cut the strip sets into (64) 2″ B-C segments as shown in Figure 3.

Figure 3
Cut the strip sets
into 2" B-C
segments.

Figure 4
Join 2 B-C segments to
complete a B-C unit.

3. Join two B-C segments to make a B-C unit as shown in Figure 4; press seam to one side. Repeat to make 32 B-C units. Set aside remaining B-C segments.

4. Sew an A square to a B-C unit as shown in Figure 5; press seam toward A. Repeat for 24 pieced units.

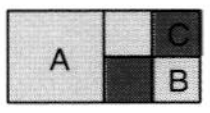

Figure 5
Sew A to a B-C unit.

5. Join two pieced units to complete one Double Four-Patch block referring to the block drawing for positioning; press seam in one direction. Repeat for 12 blocks.

Completing the Pieced Center

1. Join two Four-Patch and two Double Four-Patch blocks to make a block row as shown in Figure 6; press seams toward the Four-Patch blocks. Repeat for four rows, again referring to Figure 6 for positioning of blocks.

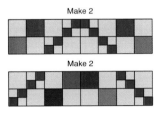

Make 2

Make 2

Figure 6
Join blocks in rows.

2. Join two B-C units as shown in Figure 7; press seam to one side. Repeat for four units.

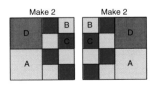

Make 2   Make 2

Figure 7
Join 2 B-C units;
sew to an A-D unit.

3. Join a pieced unit with an A-D unit to complete a pieced square, again referring to Figure 7; press seam toward A-D. Repeat for four pieced squares, again referring to Figure 7 for positioning of units.

4. Join two pieced squares with two Double Four-Patch blocks to make a block row as shown in Figure 8; press seams in one direction. Repeat for two rows.

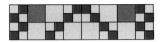

Figure 8
Join pieced squares with
blocks to make a block row.

5. Join the rows to complete the pieced center referring to the Placement Diagram for positioning of rows; press seams in one direction.

Adding Borders

1. Sew E to opposite long sides and F to the top and bottom of the pieced center; press seams toward strips.

2. Sew G to opposite long sides and H to the top and bottom of the pieced center; press seams toward strips.

3. Sew I to opposite long sides and J to the top and bottom of the pieced center; press seams toward strips.

4. Join the K/N/O strips on short ends to make a long strip; press seams in one direction. Cut into two 51½" K strips, two 59" N strips and two 48½" O strips.

5. Sew K to opposite long sides and L to the top and bottom of the pieced center; press seams toward strips.

6. Sew M to opposite sides of A as shown in Figure 9; press seams toward M. Repeat for four A-M units.

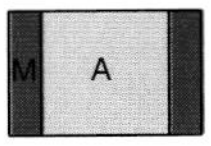

Figure 9
Sew M to opposite
sides of A.

7. Join eight A-D units with one A-M unit to make a side border strip as shown in Figure 10; press seams toward D. Repeat for two strips.

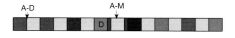

Figure 10
Complete a side border strip.

8. Sew a side border strip to opposite long sides of the pieced center; press seams toward K strips.

9. Join six A-D units with one A-M unit and two D squares to make an end border strip as shown in Figure 11; press seams toward D. Repeat for two strips.

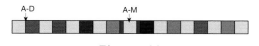

Figure 11
Complete an end border strip.

10. Sew an end border strip to the top and bottom of the pieced center; press seams toward L strips.

11. Sew N to opposite long sides and O to the top and bottom of the pieced center; press seams toward strips.

12. Join the P/Q strips on short ends to make a long strip; press seams in one direction. Cut into two 60½" P strips and two 54½" Q strips.

13. Sew P to opposite long sides and Q to the top and bottom of the pieced center; press seams toward strips.

Completing Appliqué
1. Trace the R–W appliqué shapes on the paper side of the fusible web referring to patterns for number to trace and leaving a margin around each shape. Cut out each shape, leaving a margin around marked shape; remove unmarked paper line.

2. Arrange shapes on the wrong side of fabrics referring to the patterns for correct fabrics; fuse. Remove remaining paper. ***Note:*** *Cut the T and W pieces from the same plaid fat quarter. Cut the R and two U pieces from another plaid fat quarter and the remaining U pieces from the other seven plaid fat quarters.*

3. Center an R-S-T motif on each cream plaid I strip and a U-V-W motif on each cream plaid J

strip referring to the Placement Diagram and quilt photo for positioning.

4. Join two olive/red plaid bias vine strips with a diagonal seam referring to instructions on page 60; press seam open. Repeat to make four strips.

5. Arrange one vine strip between an R-S-T motif and a U-V-W motif, making a loop in the border corner, trimming excess at each end and tucking ends under the appliqué motifs as shown in Figure 12.

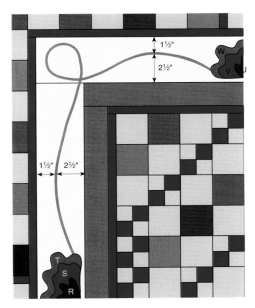

Figure 12
Arrange a vine strip
from motif to motif.

6. When satisfied with positioning, apply thin line of basting glue under vine strip to hold in place; repeat on all corners of the I/J borders.

7. Arrange seven plaid U pieces along each vine strip referring to the Placement Diagram and close-up photo for positioning.

8. Place a red U piece in each corner loop, again referring to the Placement Diagram and close-up photo for position.

9. When satisfied with positioning, fuse all appliqué pieces in place.

10. Using black all-purpose thread in the top and bobbin and a medium-width buttonhole stitch, stitch around edges of all appliqué pieces and vines to complete the appliqué.

Finishing the Quilt
1. Complete the quilt referring to Finishing the Quilt on page 9. ▪

Framed in Plaid Flowers
Placement Diagram
54" x 66"

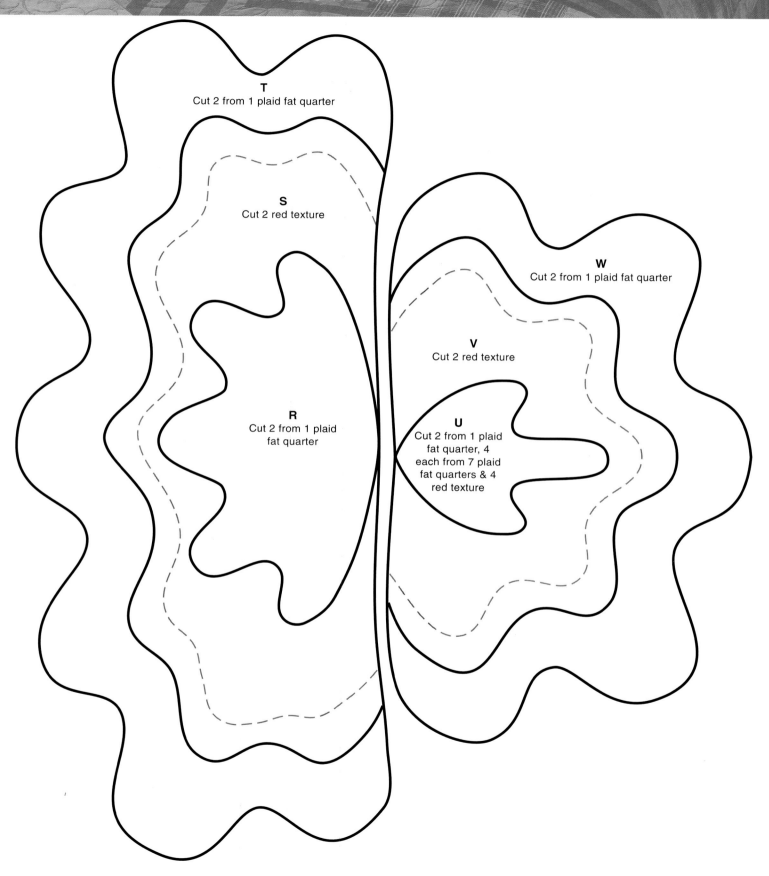

T
Cut 2 from 1 plaid fat quarter

S
Cut 2 red texture

W
Cut 2 from 1 plaid fat quarter

V
Cut 2 red texture

R
Cut 2 from 1 plaid fat quarter

U
Cut 2 from 1 plaid fat quarter, 4 each from 7 plaid fat quarters & 4 red texture

Firecracker Basket

BY SUE HARVEY

Plaid dimensional embellishments combine with a patriotic stripe in this small wall quilt.

Project Specifications
Skill Level: Intermediate
Quilt Size: 20" x 22"

Fabric & Batting
- ⅛ yard gold plaid
- ½ yard blue plaid
- ½ yard stripe
- ⅝ yard red plaid
- ⅝ yard cream plaid
- Backing 22" x 24"
- Batting 22" x 24"

Supplies & Tools
- All-purpose thread to match fabrics
- Quilting thread
- Red and blue 6-strand embroidery floss
- 4 (⅞") blue buttons
- 4 (⅝") red buttons
- 6 (½") red buttons
- 2" x 12" strip fusible web
- 2 (10") red chenille strips
- Spray bottle
- Stiff-bristle brush
- Basic tools and supplies and masking tape

Cutting
1. Cut one strip cream plaid 9" by width of fabric; subcut into one 9" A square and two 6⅞" D squares. Cut one D square in half on one diagonal.

2. Cut three strips cream plaid 1½" by width of fabric; subcut into two 12½" F strips, two 16½" H strips and two 14½" J strips.

3. Cut one strip cream plaid 2½" by width of fabric; subcut into two 14½" G strips.

4. Cut one strip red plaid 3⅞" by width of fabric; subcut into one 3⅞" E square and four 3⅜" C squares.

5. Cut eight strips red plaid 1½" by width of fabric; subcut into four 14½" K strips and four 16½" I strips.

6. Cut one strip blue plaid 3½" by width of fabric; subcut into four 3½" L squares.

7. Cut two strips blue plaid ½" by width of fabric for gathered strips.

8. Cut three strips blue plaid 2¼" by width of fabric for binding.

9. Cut one 9⅜" x 9⅜" square from striped fabric with stripe running diagonally from corner to corner; cut in half once diagonally across stripe to make two basket triangles.

Piecing Top
1. Sew a D triangle to two adjacent sides of the A square as shown in Figure 1; press seams toward D.

Figure 1
Sew D to 2 adjacent
sides of A.

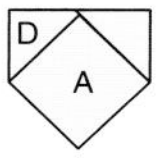

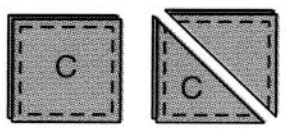

Figure 2
Stitch all around outside
edge of layered C squares;
cut in half on 1 diagonal.

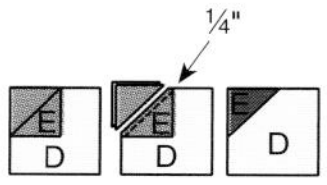

Figure 5
Place E on 1 corner of D.

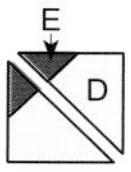

Figure 6
Cut D-E in half along the
diagonal of E to complete
the basket feet pieces.

2. Place two C squares right sides together; stitch all around outside edge using a ¼" seam allowance as shown in Figure 2. Repeat with remaining C squares.

3. Cut each layered square in half on one diagonal, again referring to Figure 2. Trim corner seam allowances; turn triangles right side out and press flat.

4. Arrange the triangles along the long edge of one basket triangle, leaving a ⅜" margin at each side edge and aligning center V of triangles with center of the basket triangle as shown in Figure 3. Pin in place. Baste ⅛" from top edge.

Figure 3
Arrange triangles along
edge of 1 basket triangle.

5. Place the second basket triangle right sides together with the basted triangle with C triangles between; pin in place. Stitch along top edge with ¼" seam allowance as shown in Figure 4. Press the top basket triangle to the back to complete the basket base. Topstitch ¼" from top edge of triangles to hold flat.

Figure 4
Stitch along top edge of
layered basket triangles.

6. Draw a diagonal line from corner to corner on the wrong side of the E square. Place on one corner of the remaining D square as shown in Figure 5. Stitch on the marked line; trim seam allowance to ¼" and press E to the right side.

7. Cut the D-E square in half along the E diagonal to complete the basket feet pieces as shown in Figure 6.

8. Apply the fusible web strip to the wrong side of the gold fabric; cut out. Cut one ¼" x 12" strip and two ¼" x 10" strips from the fused strip. Remove paper backing.

9. Place the 12" strip along the center diagonal of the A square, beginning ¼" below the seam intersection of the D triangles as shown in Figure 7. Place the 10" strips on each side of the center strip, again referring to Figure 7. Fuse strips in place.

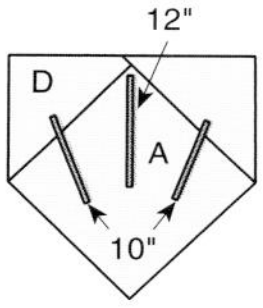

Figure 7
Place the 12" and 10"
fused strips on A.

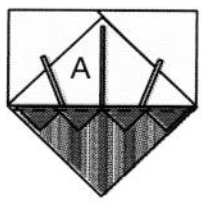

Figure 8
Place the basket base
on the A square.

10. Place the basket base on the bottom half of the A square, matching edges as shown in Figure 8; pin in place. **Note:** *Do not stitch top edge; it should remain open to insert embellishments.*

11. Stitch the D-E triangles to adjacent sides of the basket base/A unit as shown in Figure 9; press seams toward D-E triangles.

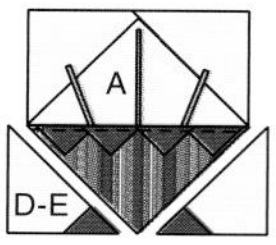

Figure 9
Stitch D-E triangles to
adjacent sides of the
basket base/A unit.

12. Sew the F strips to opposite sides and the G strips to the top and bottom of the center unit.

13. Sew an H strip between two I strips; press seams toward I. Repeat for two strips. Sew a pieced strip to opposite sides of the center unit; press seams toward pieced strips.

14. Sew a J strip between two K strips; press seams toward K. Repeat for two strips. Sew an L square to each end of each pieced strip; press seams toward the pieced strips. Sew a strip to the top and bottom of the center unit; press seams toward strips.

Completing the Quilt

1. Complete the quilt referring to Finishing the Quilt on page 9, leaving the top edge of the basket piece open.

Adding Dimensional Embellishments

1. Trace 15 star point pieces on the wrong side of the gold fabric, arranging them along one edge and leaving ⅜" between pieces.

2. Fold fabric in half with right sides together to make a double strip with traced pieces on top as shown in Figure 10.

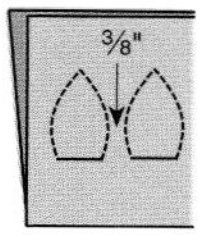

Figure 10
Trace star points on 1 edge leaving ⅜" between pieces; fold fabric in half.

3. Stitch along curved edges of each point, leaving straight bottom unstitched.

4. Cut out each piece leaving a ⅛" seam allowance around the stitched edges. Trim the point seam allowance; turn right side out.

5. Using a doubled, knotted length of gold thread, gather five star point pieces on the thread as shown in Figure 11. Knot at end; join two end pieces to form a star shape, again referring to Figure 11. Repeat to make three stars.

Figure 11
Gather 5 star points on thread; join ends to form star shape.

6. Place a star on the end of each fused gold plaid strip; hand-stitch in place.

7. Measure 16" from end of each of the ½"-wide blue plaid strips and 9" from the other end as shown in Figure 12.

16"   9"

Figure 12
Measure 16" from 1 end and 9" from other end.

8. Using a long machine stitch and gold thread, backstitch at beginning end and stitch from the end to a mark. Stop stitching and cut thread, leaving ends long enough to pull. Repeat on remaining end of strip as shown in Figure 13.

Figure 13
Stitch from end to mark on each end of strip.

9. Gather each end of strip as shown in Figure 14; knot ends. Cut strip in ungathered section to make one 8"-long strip and one 6"-long strip, again referring to Figure 14. Repeat with second strip.

Figure 14
Gather ends of strip; cut strip in ungathered section.

10. Arrange the shorter strips on the outside of the star/strip motifs and the longer strips between the star/strip motifs, placing ungathered ends inside the basket.

11. Using 3 strands blue embroidery floss, attach a ⅝" red button to the top and at the basket edge of the longer gathered strips and a ½" red button to the top and basket edge of the shorter gathered strips and to the center of the longer gathered strips. Leave floss ends ¼" long.

12. Using 6 strands red embroidery floss, attach a ⅞" blue button in the center of each star and on the center intersection of the red triangles on the basket. Leave floss ends ⅝" long.

13. Cut one chenille strip in half and the other strip into three pieces. Arrange the longer pieces around the basket base and feet; stitch in place according to manufacturer's instructions. Arrange the shorter pieces on the star/strip motifs; stitch in place.

14. Place masking tape pieces under edges of stitched chenille strips to protect background fabric and fused strip pieces as shown in Figure 15.

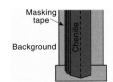

Figure 15
Place masking tape under edges of chenille strips.

15. Brush chenille pieces slightly; spray with water and brush to completely fluff out; remove masking tape pieces. Use masking tape to clean any chenille threads and lint from background. ■

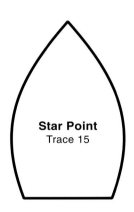

Star Point
Trace 15

Firecracker Basket
Placement Diagram
20" x 22"

Preparing Bias Strips

Add interest to quilt edges or vines to appliqué motifs with plaid or striped bias strips.

Cutting Bias Strips

Using fabric-width strip cut in specific project instructions, unfold strip and press flat. Trim selvage edge from left end. Place 45-degree-angle line of ruler along bottom edge of fabric strip and align ruler edge with upper left corner.

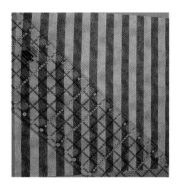

Rotary-cut along edge of ruler to remove a right triangle (bottom left corner), leaving a true bias fabric edge.

Align bias edge with appropriate measurement on ruler as directed in project instructions for width of bias strips; cut strip.

Continue to cut strips from bias edge referring to project instructions for number of strips needed.

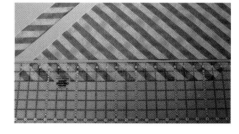

To cut more than one layer of fabric at a time, press each strip flat and layer strips with right sides up. Trim selvage edge from left end of layered unit. Trim corner and cut strips from bias edge.

Do not cut strips from a folded strip or from strips that are layered right or wrong sides together. Each cut will yield a bias strip and a reverse bias strip. When using a plaid or stripe, the direction of the plaid or stripe will be reversed from strip to strip.

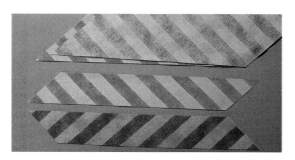

Strips that are cut in reverse will also have ends that will need to be trimmed square before joining. Trimming reduces the length of each strip by twice the width of the strip. For example, if the strip is 2½" x 21", the trimmed strip will be only 16" long.

Joining Bias Strips

Place two bias strips right sides together with diagonal ends offset to leave a ¼" seam allowance at the notched intersection of the strips.

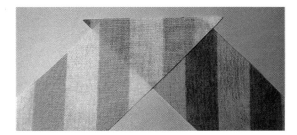

Stitch from notch to notch across ends of strips using a ¼" seam allowance. Trim small triangle "ears" at each end. Press seam to one side.

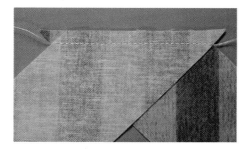

Continue to join strips as directed for specific project. ∎

Matching Stripes at Mitered Corners

When a stripe meets at a mitered corner, the stripes should match.

To make a stripe match perfectly at a mitered corner requires advance planning. Begin by choosing the area of the stripe to be used and then cut identical strips for borders.

To cut identical strips, place the rotary ruler with the half-strip measurement in the center of the chosen stripe section. For example, in the example shown a 3"-wide stripe section was chosen, so the center of the stripe is 1½". Place the ruler with the 1½" line in the center of the chosen stripe section and make one cut.

Turn the strip and repeat with the 1½" mark on the stripe center and cut again. You should have a 3"-wide strip with the chosen area centered. Repeat for four identical strips.

Sew a strip to each side of the pieced center or block, stopping stitching ¼" from the edge of the pieced top and secure; press seams toward strips. At this point you have excess unstitched at each end.

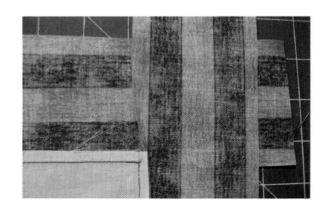

Lay the pieced center or block on a flat surface; fold the top strip back on itself at a 45-degree angle and check to be sure that the stripes match at the fold.

Turn over to check for matching; trim seam allowance to ¼" and press seam open to complete the mitered corner. Repeat on all corners. ■

If you have a perfect match, press to mark a crease. Turn the corner over and check to see that the stripes still match.

Fold the quilt top, matching edges of strips with creased line on top; turn corner seam allowances back to expose stitching and pin to hold. Stitch on the creased line to complete the mitered seam.

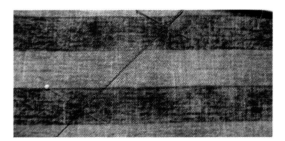

Metric Conversion Charts

Metric Conversions

U.S. Measurements		Multiplied by		Metric Measurement
yards	x	.9144	=	meters (m)
yards	x	91.44	=	centimeters (cm)
inches	x	2.54	=	centimeters (cm)
inches	x	25.40	=	millimeters (mm)
inches	x	.0254	=	meters (m)

Metric Measurements		Multiplied by		U.S. Measurements
centimeters	x	.3937	=	inches
meters	x	1.0936	=	yards

Standard Equivalents

U.S. Measurement		Metric Measurement		
1/8 inch	=	3.20 mm	=	0.32 cm
1/4 inch	=	6.35 mm	=	0.635 cm
3/8 inch	=	9.50 mm	=	0.95 cm
1/2 inch	=	12.70 mm	=	1.27 cm
5/8 inch	=	15.90 mm	=	1.59 cm
3/4 inch	=	19.10 mm	=	1.91 cm
7/8 inch	=	22.20 mm	=	2.22 cm
1 inch	=	25.40 mm	=	2.54 cm
1/8 yard	=	11.43 cm	=	0.11 m
1/4 yard	=	22.86 cm	=	0.23 m
3/8 yard	=	34.29 cm	=	0.34 m
1/2 yard	=	45.72 cm	=	0.46 m
5/8 yard	=	57.15 cm	=	0.57 m
3/4 yard	=	68.58 cm	=	0.69 m
7/8 yard	=	80.00 cm	=	0.80 m
1 yard	=	91.44 cm	=	0.91 m

Fabrics & Supplies

Cardinals Rule: Checkmate II stripe and Marble Mania mottled fabric collections by Patrick Lose, Noel fabric collection by Lisa DeBee Schiller and Nature fabric collection by Herry Smith from Timeless Treasures.

Firecracker Basket: Steam-A-Seam 2 double-stick fusible web from The Warm Co., Chenille By The Inch from Fabric Café and Theresa's Hand Dyed Buttons from Hillcreek Designs

Flower Paths: Briar Rose fabric collection from RJR Fabrics

Framed in Plaid Flowers: Lite Steam-A-Seam 2 double-stick fusible web from The Warm Co. and Roxanne Glue-Baste-It!

Nosegay Stars: Victoria's Scattered Garden fabric collection from RJR Fabrics and Fabric Stabilizer spray from Sullivans

Patriotic Bouquets: Regatta fabric collection from RJR Fabrics

Plaid Maze: Checkmate II stripe by Patrick Lose and Noel fabric collection by Lisa DeBee Schiller from Timeless Treasures

Starring Stripes: Checkmate II stripe and Marble Mania mottled fabric collections by Patrick Lose from Timeless Treasures

Willy-Nilly: Brushed flannels and plaids from Marcus Brothers

Flower Paths, Starring Stripes, Firecracker Basket, Riding Around, Strips & Squares and Framed in Plaid Flowers were professionally machine-quilted by Sandy Boobar using Natural Cotton batting from Fairfield Processing.

Plaid Maze, Willy-Nilly, Patriotic Bouquets, Cardinals Rule and Nosegay Stars were professionally machine-quilted by Dianne Hodgkins using Cotton Classic batting from Fairfield Processing.

All quilts were machine-pieced or appliquéd using Star Machine Quilting Thread from Coats.

E-mail: Customer_Service @ whitebirches.com

Stripes & Plaids is published by House of White Birches, 306 East Parr Road, Berne, IN 46711, telephone (260) 589-4000. Printed in USA. Copyright © 2005 House of White Birches.

RETAILERS: If you would like to carry this pattern book or any other House of White Birches publications, call the Wholesale Department at Annie's Attic to set up a direct account: (903) 636-4303. Also, request a complete listing of publications available from House of White Birches.

Every effort has been made to ensure that the instructions in this pattern book are complete and accurate. We cannot, however, take responsibility for human error, typographical mistakes or variations in individual work.

ISBN: 1-59217-079-X
1 2 3 4 5 6 7 8 9

STAFF

Editors: Jeanne Stauffer, Sandra L. Hatch
Associate Editor: Dianne Schmidt
Technical Artist: Connie Rand
Copy Supervisor: Michelle Beck,
Copy Editors: Nicki Lehman, Mary Martin, Beverly Richardson

Graphic Arts Supervisor: Ronda Bechinski
Graphic Artists: Debby Keel, Edith Teegarden
Assistant Art Director: Nick Pierce
Photography: Tammy Christian, Carl Clark, Christena Green, Matt Owen
Photo Stylist: Tammy Nussbaum